I0416090

Everything Hurts & I Don't Know Why:
20 Tips To Help You Make Sense Of Life
By. C. Alexander

Dedication

I dedicate this book to my support system. Those who encouraged me through unconditional love and support through my bad days, and became the main characters In my healing journey.

My Wife Briana, whose love knows no bounds, and through that, I was able to feel safe enough to step out of fight or flight and into a place that allowed me to start the process. To quote our vows, "Home is anywhere you are."

My Mother Rachel. Your years of sacrifice and guidance shaped me. You're my best friend. Thank you for having me, even if I wasn't the easiest child to raise.

My Siblings. David, Roger, Sierra, Nic, Nate, Aaron, and Mya. We have an unbreakable bond and I'm thankful every day for that. You guys are my heart.

Jan. You helped me through so much in my life. I love you forever and you'll always be my family.

My aunts and uncles, without some of you, I wouldn't know my worth. I wouldn't know the potential I held. You guys stepped in when I needed it most, I'll never forget that.

My grandparents, You guys were like second parents to me. Kohnke and the Barrett side. We've lost two of you, and I know you're guiding me still. I feel you in everything I do.

My friends, new and old, make life easier to live. Rob, Chad S, Chad G, Jeff, Kit, Ruy.
 You helped me more than you know.

Finally, Julia. When we met, I was at my lowest point. Through your guidance, I was able to get to the point I am at now, Living a functional and most importantly, healthy life. I can never find the words to express what that means to me, Because you followed your calling to help others, You saved my life, and By saving mine, You helped me save countless others.

Preface

There are many times I thought I'd lose my shit. Instead, I caught my breath.
This world is full of made-up things that only serve a purpose to those looking to understand what they don't.
The unknown.
Why love will make you feel high one moment and like death the next.

The most important thing to remember above all and before the rest is nothing that you think matters does, and what you write off as trivial makes your life worth living.

Love is the most powerful force you'll ever experience. Even when it's bad. It's worth it.

The experience itself is a pivotal point in your story. Your first heartbreak, the first time you develop a crush for somebody who doesn't know you exist, your pets that you love the hell out of knowing the day will come when they no longer share your existence, childhood friends that grow up and forget about the pact you made in middle school to never part.

So what are you? And how did you end up here? In this place where nothing makes sense and there's more that could kill you than heal you.

Well, honestly we could get into that but we humans have a million theories for one thing that all end up contradicting before ending up back at the same place anyway. Besides, everything is made up, remember?

So I could give you my theories or the ideals that helped me cope in this world but let's be honest, most of you have your theories and quite honestly I in no way am trying to tell you how to think on this floating rock we inhabit.

But I can give you some tips from my personal experience on this planet that'll hopefully make this life a lot less painful.

I know some of you are thinking, "What does this guy know?!".
Yes, I may have only lived half of my life thus far but I've
experienced more pain in my short 27 years than most experience
in a lifetime.
I also took on the challenge to change the narrative for my future
children and break generational cycles. I began healing everything
that made me feel like I wanted to die.
After 15 failed attempts, a dozen toxic coping mechanisms, many
terrible relationships, 2 decades of blaming the world, and a million
excuses, I took charge of my life. I took responsibility. I decided
that I was either going to heal or die. I've had enough.
Now, I'm not saying it'll be easy and I'm not saying it'll all make
sense at the moment but, taking this journey will be the bravest
and most rewarding thing you've ever done.
Besides, what do you have to lose?

Tip 1:

Everything that hurts, makes you whole.

Although you don't remember your first breath, you've been experiencing pain since you were born. It's one of the constants of life. Depressing isn't it? Two people decide they are into each other enough to purposely or accidentally create another life and well, nobody asked your opinion on it.

So now we're here. Now what? You survived X amount of years and after experiencing whatever trauma life Cooked up for you, you're here. Still breathing...barely.

There are many different kinds of trauma. But most of us are so suffocated on our own we don't stop to think of the effect others' pain had on them. No one trauma is the same, no scar is the same, no memory the same. Even if both people were experiencing the same event.

It's like looking at art. One picture has a million different meanings.

Remember what I said about humans and their need to understand what can't be comprehended? There ya go. Case and point.

Your trauma made you and shaped you into whatever kind of person you are today. And well, you could either be your villain or your hero. It's up to you how your story plays out.

You alone are the author of your book. You control what your name means. Your legacy. And although it may be difficult to wrap your mind around, your trauma was necessary.
Let's begin with contrast. Now the definition of contracts reads as follows

"The act of contrasting; the state of being contrasted. · a striking exhibition of unlikeness. · a person or thing that is strikingly unlike in comparison"
but words are just words without a living example

that you can associate yourself with, giving the words a deeper meaning.

Contrast is comparing two things that are opposite or have nothing to do with one another. The contrast I'm going to be talking about is emotional.

Now to help you understand more practically, let's say you've watched a million love stories. You've seen the prince whisk in from his castle and save the peasant girl he fell madly in love with and have always thought "Boy, I'd kill to be her". But you've never been in love personally.

You have an idea of what love is but in a romantic sense, you have no experience to compare it to.

You learn love from your family starting as soon as you take your first breath.

Believe it or not, your definition of love started hundreds of years ago with how your ancestors were taught to love.

See every family has things they pass down to future generations, for some, it's wealth and values that honestly have no place in this day and time but their comfort to your folks, and doing them is easier than breaking the tradition. For others, it's diabetes or a trait. Some of us are so lucky we inherit the psychological traits or toxic generational cycles like abuse and addiction.

Whatever it may be, it influences your definition of love and self-worth and honestly those things color the glasses you see the world through. It starts with your developmental years of 0-7.

See during this time you learn quickly. You repeat what those around you do and get a general feel for this strange place and how to operate within it.

Going back to our example formula and putting this into an experience you can relate to, your parents may not be the most forward with emotions and the way they talk to each other may be normal to you because it's all you've known. Your dad works his life away and provides but also plays the role of enforcer.

You have a fear of your father because the only time you see him is at night when he comes home and mom tells him all you've been up to throughout the day.

Your relationship with men would most likely look like this: He provides, he isn't emotional, you don't care to find a connection within him, and you find yourself convincing yourself that your needs aren't important because well... he provides and that should be enough.

Or, we have the opposite side of the coin. You look for all of your emotional security in a relationship and when said person doesn't meet your needs you beat yourself up for it.

Now your mother was a nurturing person who dealt with the day-to-day activities and was always there to comfort you when you needed a shoulder. Mom also put up with your father's temper and made excuses for his actions that most of the time led back to her being the "problem".

Your view of women is now either that they are weak and you develop resentment or that you have to follow your mother's footsteps and put up with anything that's thrown your way as long as your partner provides.

Now we do have a special breed of people who choose to be the cure breakers and want to be nothing like their parents because they realize the toxicity of their upbringing. This in no way is an easy path but quite honestly, neither is repeating the cycle. I am one of these people. I am a curse breaker.
And if you're reading this book chances are you are too.

Let's get something straight before we dive further into this narrative. Parenting is hard. Life alone is hard and confusing and has no clear rule book or plot but adds the responsibility of guiding another into the mix.. man.

Parents make mistakes. The same way kids do. We're human. There's a 99% chance that you'll do something that influences your child in a way that you wished would've played out differently. The change comes when you realize your mistakes and take responsibility for them. Admit your imperfections and correct your behavior.

Now as I was saying, your view of the world and yourself in this world is dictated by your relationships with other people. You learn in school to cooperate with your peers and find your place in society. You'll find yourself doing things you'd never expect yourself to do for the approval of those peers and there will come a time when you don't like yourself all that much.

You've experienced contrast. You notice your family is unlike others or a lot like others. You notice your hair or skin or appearance isn't like others or you'll conform to fit in. Whatever path you take, it was always based on environmental influence and you didn't even notice. You just did it.

We need to be accepted by our peers. Were group-minded people. When you don't feel seen, heard, and celebrated you rebel and blame the world for your feelings of self-hatred. Some people act out in terrible ways and hurt a lot of people in the process. They wanted their pain to be felt.

When the description of you from others' mouths contradicts your description of self, you have this inner battle.
If you don't know who you are, others will tell you.
That feeling never really leaves you. It just forms around whatever person you grow into, good or bad; you're always left with this void that you can't seem to fill.
I mean you'll try to.

You'll form toxic habits that feel good until they don't. You'll find yourself in a chaotic tornado that follows you everywhere you go.

The chaos is only there until you notice the contrast. Your life will get these situations that pop up like a speeding freight train and knock you down over and over until the root trauma is called out and worked through.
You don't love yourself because you didn't feel accepted by your peers or you didn't get the nurturing or protection you needed as a child. We're programmed to blame ourselves or worse, blame everyone else for how we feel.

You've heard the stories. A man works his life away and looks up 20 years later hating everyone and everything. Gets tired of it all, wonders where he went wrong and either calls it quits or makes drastic changes that don't make sense to the ones that have known him forever.

He got stuck in the cycle of life. It's incredibly easy to do. You lived for the approval of your parents, then your peers, then your spouse, then your kids.

Do any of us truly know who the hell we are?
If you don't know who you are, others will tell you.

The moral of the story, it's not all your fault but what happened shaped you into who you are today. When you become aware of that fact, it's now a choice to continue down that path or to choose to take another.

Let your pain fuel you. If you're unhappy, make a change.
Life is made up of a billion choices. Make a new one. It's your life anyway. Even if it seems impossible, it isn't. Even if you have no idea how to start.
Understand your trauma, and change your life.

1   Chapter Points to remember

- No one trauma is the same
- You're trauma shaped you
- Contrast is necessary
- Your family taught you how to love
- Let your pain fuel you

Tip 2:

When they say they won't, they will.

Everyone will hurt you. Get comfortable with that uncomfortable fact. They might not mean to, or like that they did. But they will let you down at least once.

What happens is, we have this internal need to connect. We have 3 main emotional needs when trying to live an emotionally healthy life.

1. To be seen
2. To be heard
3. To be celebrated

When those aren't met. We develop insecurities and find ourselves filling those voids with things that feel good but turn our life upside down.

We have these ideas or expectations if you will, that we set for the open roles we have in our lives. Way before the face meets the role, we have an idea of how they're supposed to fit.

When they don't fit, we hate them for it.

You fall in love with someone, they show you who they are and you see a project.
No matter how hard you push or influence them, they are still them.
The fights get worse, and you look for somebody to blame. Most of the time, you blame yourself.

"Why didn't I see the signs"
"Everything was a lie"

No, they showed you who they were and you didn't believe them.

When we set standards for other people we aren't accepting them for who they are. We blame them for not fitting into our pre-made box and make them an enemy.

When they show you their true colors, believe them. It's not your fault for loving them, it's not theirs for not being the healthiest person for you in that stage of your life.

Asking somebody to change when they aren't ready is like eating a meal before it's done cooking.
They love you so when you ask them to make a promise, they do. Even though they know deep in their heart they aren't ready to make that change.
The love is real. They just aren't at the stage of growth you're asking them to be at.
Maybe one day they will be. Those promises won't be kept, and that's okay.

These experiences come into our lives to help us grow. Without these experiences, you wouldn't truly understand what you identify with and what isn't for you.

If you're unaware of the patterns you keep repeating, and how your trauma influences your daily life, you just react to the world around you out of patterns that are stored In your subconscious mind.

Most people take the route that serves them more. They act selfishly. Aside from the fact that like yourself, others also act out their trauma patterns subconsciously.

Most people are just bopping around trying to figure out life.
Young, old, it makes no difference. We're all just trying to make
the best of a historically bad situation.
It doesn't mean they don't have some good inside them, or that
they don't feel the way they said they do. They're just being true to
themselves. We do what's comfortable.

People are either a blessing or a lesson. In my experience, the
lesson is a true blessing.
Because of this experience, you got closer to knowing who you are.
What you will and won't accept for yourself. Your blessing was the
experience, even if you don't see it like that at the moment.

2   Chapter Points to remember

- We set expectations for those filling roles in our lives
- Asking someone to change before they are ready is like eating an undercooked meal
- These experiences help us grow
- We react to our world based on learned patterns
- You're blessing was the experience

Tip 3:

If it doesn't matter, what's the point?

Everything around you excluding natural creations started in the mind of another human. An idea, an inspiration. Normal flesh and blood humans just like you. Humans got this world, made it theirs, and set the rules. You just came late to The game.
So if everything is a creation, (including you if you'd like to), why does any of this matter?
Well imagine you're a video game character, and you're aware of the world around you. You know the characters, the scenes, the plot.
To you this world is real.
The players in the game know their 3D world as the real world. You as a game character believe your world is real.
If it's in your reality, it's real.
It's your perception that dictates your truth.

One thing that you can always count on, is that everything changes. Change is the most constant element in life. it's not your job to stop those changes.
Although you can dictate your own, you can't stop the wheels from turning. You just adjust.

Adjusting can be scary. We have this inner need to control our situations that 9 times out of 10 we couldn't control anyway. Adjusting or "going with the flow", gives you an advantage over the common person.

You can look at your situation and act. Where others would sink into that oh-so-familiar dark hole of depression.
Now I'm not saying depression is anyone's fault. I've struggled with it for years, but what I am saying is although you can't control what others do, you CAN control how you react to their actions.

You are the only one in control of your emotions and actions. When people are being who they are and projecting their bad feelings onto you, it's not your job to pick up those burdens.

Don't take it personally and keep it moving.
Now we humans also have this annoying trait that tells us "If I can't label it, I don't know how to approach it".
We label things to categorize them. So we know how to interact with said person or thing. If we just let things be, accept that some things we won't understand, and keep it moving, the stress goes away.

We're all just here trying to make sense of the most incomprehensible situation. When people go through their phases remember, that they're just trying to be okay.

Now as we said before, humans imagined most of this reality were all collectively a part of. So the one who created it, or holds the most power within it, sets the rules.

Now I'm not saying the one who has the power is always right.
History will teach you that when enough people disagree with the
current set of rules, we fight to change them.

Those fights had to happen. Enough people noticed that something
didn't align with them and fought for peace. The power shifted.
They believed in themselves and the common good enough to know
they were going to make changes or die trying.

Reacting and acting are not the same.
When you react, it's a subconscious movement. If somebody jumps
out at you, you'd jump.
But to act is a deliberate movement. You've thought about your
action, you've planned and executed.

Reacting is second nature. We all have typical reactions based upon
past life experiences and current emotional states.
Don't beat yourself up for reacting, but get into the habit of being
deliberate

will give you a much better outcome in this world.

Say what you mean. Your feelings are valid and you don't need the approval of others to feel the way you do. That doesn't give you the right to interfere or dictate others' emotions though. Honor your emotions and process how you feel.

Feel everything for what it is. Also, give others the same space to do it as well.
You'll start seeing changes, small ones at first. You'll notice you're more in control of your emotions, thoughts, and outcomes.
Remember, everything changes. How you feel right now isn't permanent, it's just a reaction to your world.

3   Chapter Points to remember

- Everything started as a thought
- Everything changes, and that's okay
- Going with the flow gives you an advantage
- You control how you react
- Reacting and acting are not the same thing

Tip 4:

Your thoughts matter

Now we're going to be diving deeper into what
we touched on in the last section.
Your thoughts control your outcome.

Your thoughts are so powerful that they can change the projectile
of your entire day, and If you let them fester long enough, your life.
Let's say you have a family member that is always negative when
they call you, it may be valid due to the history of your relationship
but if every time they called you, you get this dreadful feeling that
comes over you and you expect them to be the same as they always
have been.

That's exactly what they'll bring to you every time you answer the
phone.
Try being neutral in the situation. Not setting an expectation for
the call but instead staying within your peaceful emotional state.

You'd be surprised at the way the conversation goes.

Now thought is not the only element you need to consider when attempting to change or create your outside world.
The biggest piece you must remember to align first would be your emotions.
Your emotional state has the biggest impact on your life.

If you're in chaos in your head, your life will reflect that.
Before attempting to create you must come back to self.
Coming back to self isn't as easy as one may think, at first.

Start by making a list of things that make you feel good.
Activities or thoughts that make you feel at peace and as if nothing could go wrong.
When you're attempting to come back to yourself, pick from the list and do that activity or put yourself back in that memory.

Now when you feel that peace comes over you. That feeling of calm. You're ready to start.

Step 1:
Get comfortable somewhere where you won't be bothered.

Step 2:
Focus your thoughts on positive things. Those can include people you love, places that make you feel safe, your pets, etc.

Step 3:
Once you get to a place where you feel your peace settling in, imagine the things you want to happen in your reality. Things or people you want to interact with. Think about this person or thing down to the smallest detail.

Step 4:
Imagine yourself interacting with this person or thing. How would it feel to drive it, own it, see it, love it

Step 5: let yourself sit in that space until you feel no difference between your reality and your creation. Feel as if it already exists for you. Carry that feeling.

Step 6:
Know that it is done. And let it go.

It's okay to come back to the thought but don't allow yourself to obsess over it. You set your intention now you're waiting for inspiration to strike.

When the inspiration strikes, it might not make sense at first but just trust, and act.
Most things end up coming in ways you wouldn't even imagine.
Don't limit yourself to one path of delivery.
Let go and know it is done.

Congrats you just learned manifestation.

Mindset is everything. Going back to the classic "Glass half empty, half full" quote. Two people can see the same thing and interpret it in two completely different ways.

It is your choice when perception comes into play. It is always your choice.

If you think everything is doom and gloom. That's exactly what you'll get.
If you let things happen and go with the ebb and flow of life, remain in a positive mindset even if your external world doesn't reflect it yet, it will adjust to your view.

This works on everything. Humans included.
Send love to all, and love will find its way back to you. It's the natural order of things.

Having a positive view on things isn't the only component though. The other side of the coin is your attitude.
If you believe all things are always working out for you, they will.
If you Carry the emotion that everything is trying to destroy you, nobody understands you. That's what you'll get.
Practice makes perfect. You'll get it. Remember why you started.

4   Chapter Points to remember

- Thoughts control your outcome
- Your emotional state matters
- Manifestation steps
- Act when inspired
- It is always your choice

Tip 5:

Don't sweat the small stuff

My late grandmother loved this quote. This was her go-to saying when she could feel you were upset about something.
This quote simply means, don't let yourself make a mountain out of a molehill.

If you allow yourself to get worked up over small things, you'll waste all of your energy on situations that would have otherwise been tiny.

Not everything deserves a reaction. Not everything deserves your energy or attention. Choose your battles, or they'll all choose you.

By focusing on all these battles you've decided were worth your time, you end up missing out on life. You'll spend all of your time worked up and afraid of your own shadow.

You'll have issues maintaining healthy relationships and wonder why you feel so alone.

Misery loves company. I can promise it's a visitor you don't want. Besides, time flies.

Life is but a blink of an eye. Most only get a maximum of 100 years and although some, including myself, believe that you come back, in this life, this body, you have one shot. Make it worth it.

Remember, don't get caught up in trivial things, stay present. If it pops up, you are fully capable of handling it. You've handled worse.

When you're living through your day-to-day routine, everything seems huge. When you're in the moment and dealing with multiple things at once, it's very easy to feel overwhelmed.

As hard as it is to do, taking a step back and evaluating the situation as if it's happening around you and not to you.

When you separate yourself from the situation it allows you to look at it from a different perspective. Looking at the situation in a detached way has its advantages.

1. We tend to give others better advice than we give ourselves.
2. Were able to take some of the emotional weight out of the decision-making.

It can seem silly to you as you're living through these situations but trust me, learning to detach and evaluate can save you from a lot of stress and heartache. Your energy is like money, don't give it to anyone who asks for it.

5   Chapter Points to remember

- Don't make a mountain out of a molehill
- Not everything deserves a reaction
- Misery loves company
- Stay present
- Evaluate as if it's happening around you, not to you

Tip 6:

The cycle of all things

There is an ebb and flow to life. We like to get caught up in the ebb.
The movement. Sometimes this river of life feels like a tsunami.
As the cycle goes through, everything has a polarity. Not a good
and bad side but different degrees of the same thing.
Different intensities or "degrees" if you will.
What goes up, must come down.
Sunshine comes after the rain.
Every famous quote that has been passed down to us all has a
similar theme.
The bad times don't last, but sunshine won't either.
Enjoy every great moment, truly be present in it. Soak it in. When
the storm starts brewing and you feel your feet slipping, move.
Go with the changes. You can't expect to sit in your car without
moving it and expect to be at your destination, can you?
The same goes for life. If you keep wishing for

things to change without taking the steps to make it happen, you're going to wish yourself out of life.

Now change is scary. It's uncomfortable and it makes you feel uneasy.
All of those points are valid ones.
That doesn't mean you don't have what it takes to do it anyway though. The change will happen with or without you, and If your stuck in the past, it's like being stuck in the 80s while living in the 2020s.

Your body changes many times throughout your life. Your mindset, bone structure, cells, tastes, likes, and dislikes.
You aren't the same person you were when you were younger. You went with the natural changes that life handed you and adjusted.

You've already done this before. When you try to apply the same concept to your everyday life, that's where the fear comes in.

You got this. Just breathe. Adjust and know this is just the cycle of all things.
Like waves in the ocean.
Everything has a cycle to keep things harmonious.

6   Chapter Points to remember

- Ebb and flow, movement and change
- When you feel your feet slipping, move
- Take steps toward your goal
- Change is scary but important
- Adjust and know your safe

Tip 7:

If you don't learn the first time, you'll learn the 10th

Life lessons pop up in different ways. Most commonly, Through your relationships.
Now I'm not trying to put us all back on that dark thought train of exes and failed friendships, but even the worst ones were important.

See after the programming ages of 0-7 the only way we learn afterward is through trauma or repetition.
If you touch a hot stove, you don't have to go around touching every stove to know fire burns.
Sometimes this concept gets complicated.
Popular life lessons include self-worth, setting healthy boundaries, believing in yourself, etc.
The way these lessons manifest in your life is different for every person.

Think back to your worst relationship. The one that tested you in every possible way.
While you were going through it, it felt like hell. You fell in love with somebody who was brought into your life to push you to the edge, push you in ways you wouldn't have imagined were possible.

Let's say this person was controlling. Let's say they told you how to act and think.
You love them so you went along with it
The lesson In this relationship was boundaries and self-worth.

You had to experience this contrast to understand what was and wasn't for you.
You got to the point where you had enough. You picked your head up and stood up for yourself, as hard as it was, you did it.

You vowed to never fall victim to another. Now if you didn't understand the lesson in this you may have blamed the person for acting the way they did, you thought it was just them. You get into another relationship similar to this one but far worse.

If you don't see the lesson, you repeat it. Every time it comes in, it's worse.

That example may have been harsh and triggering for some people. If it wasn't harsh, I don't feel you'd grasp the concept. Life is real, trauma is real, and we can try to run and hide from it but that doesn't mean these things don't exist.

I've been in that place. I've been on the receiving end of toxic wrath.
At the time I blamed them. I kept repeating this cycle throughout my life. The biggest one I still deal with is self-worth. I'm a work in progress, just like you.

"It's just like riding a bike".
That can be both good and bad.
The more you do something, the easier it gets. You can push forward and fight for yourself or you can get so used to the toxicity that it becomes your normal.
Different degrees of the same thing.

Think about the big situations in your life. Take your emotions out of it and view it

like you're watching a movie trailer.
Now move to the next.
Notice any similarities?
What's the plot of the movie?

Take some time to think about this and you'll find a common theme among them.

I imagine your thinking, what if I don't want to learn lessons? Well, to this point I've found the only way out is through. If you figure out another way to get back to yourself without going through the experience, let me know will ya?

7 Chapter Points to remember

- Life lessons are common in relationships
- The worst ones were the most important
- Trauma or repetition equals learning
- Contrast taught you about yourself
- If you don't learn, you repeat

Tip 8:

The right thing often sucks

Doing the right thing when no one else gets it is one of the hardest choices to make. Standing up for the little guy, calling out things that are unfair, setting boundaries, and leaving an unhealthy situation.

Were made to be with one another. We have an inner need to belong to something. For some, that can hurt us more than help us.

One thing to remember is, that following your inner voice may be difficult but your internal guidance system is set up for a reason.

Your internal guidance system is that gut feeling you get when you know something is true. That feeling that tells you someone is lying or that something is about to happen.

When you're driving and get the push to take a different route. Listen to that voice. It'll guide you through all of life's challenges. Most of us just ignore it.

Changes come when someone realizes it needs to happen. History shows us that no one great was agreed with.

Although we know what the right or most logical move would be, we allow our emotions to make our choices for us. If we didn't allow emotions to cloud our judgment, most of us would be in a much better place in our lives.

Relationships are important. As is the need to be liked by those in relationship with us.
Most of us are guilty of letting how we feel about someone influence our decision-making when it comes to them but like I've always said, once you wake up to something, it's impossible to go back to sleep.

Practicing putting yourself and your needs first will help you in many ways, especially when it comes to doing the right thing. The 'right' thing for you may not be the 'right' thing for someone else but you have to remember the goal is peace.

What would help you manifest your peace the easiest way? What steps would be involved if you were advising a friend or a colleague? Write down the advice as if you're writing a letter to someone else and follow it.

It may seem strange at first, but the right thing often does.

8 Chapter Points to remember

- Our inner need to belong to something
- Your internal guidance system
- Change comes when you realize it needs to
- Putting yourself first
- Manifesting your peace

Tip 9:

Your dream doesn't die, it gets suffocated

Getting lost in life is almost an expected occurrence. You start life with a big imagination. Wondering how everything works and what makes it all tick. You get lost in thought and stay amazed by the colors and patterns that make up the world around you.
As you grow and settle into this strange place, you're given a set of rules.

These rules were created by the group of people around you. What you do and don't do, how to conduct yourself, how you're supposed to react to situations, and even how you're supposed to speak.

Now you will go through a phase or two that pushes every boundary and drives the ones you love nuts, but that's expected.

You also get these rules from your peers. School mates, co-workers, etc.
You want to be a part of the community so you abide by these rules even if they challenge the rules set in place by your family unit.

That'll be a challenging time for you. Going against your family unit and deciding to follow the rules set up by your peers. This may cause fights. Your family may say they don't know who you are anymore. This is all normal.

It's called being a teenager. You'll start to discover who you are and find your identity in the world. You won't be in your parent's home forever and you must discover these things about yourself.

Your tastes will change as you grow and get more experience but while that's happening, it can feel lonely.

You'll get sucked into life and feel as if you have to live up to the expectations others set for you. Go to college, or work to support the family. I had to go with the second option personally.

The thing is though, that burning passion you have for a specific thing, that thing that you've spent countless hours fantasizing about and getting lost in, doesn't go away when life sucks you in. It suffocates.

You bottle this dream up and keep telling yourself that one day you'll come back to it. Most never do. Time goes by and your "why" changes. Your "why" used to be your place in the world, then it became your responsibility to your family, that part never really changed.

You stayed there.
You feel this void that you try to fill with personal accomplishments. Nice house, car, 2.5 kids.
While your dream falls to the wayside.

The funny thing about life though, is you'll always seem to find a way back to it.
When you get wrapped up in life and feel a void, the most expected next step would be developing a hate for your situation.

It's not the people involved, you care for them. The job isn't terrible, it just doesn't ignite you. You love yourself, but you don't feel like your true self.
You feel stuck because you were gifted with the passion and inspiration to accomplish something amazing and swallowed it.

It's never too late. Yes, maybe the flame for being a famous rock star isn't as bright as it was, but teaching kids music, managing an act, or just making music because you enjoy it will still fulfill your desires.

If you love something, do it. It may not be in the same form it started in.

9 Chapter Points to remember

- Rules are created by those around you
- Going against the grain is a right of passage
- Everything about you changes as you grow, and that's normal
- Your dream will always find its way back to you
- Your dream can take on different forms

Tip 10:

Your heart doesn't store pain, your brain does

Think of your brain as a computer program.
It has the base functions that it was programmed to perform. When we experience trauma at an early age, these programs change.
When you experience trauma, your subconscious is soaking in all of the cause and effect. These actions become a pattern or a "Trauma Response".

Many have heard the saying "the heart wants, what the heart wants" or " a head over heart decision".
In reality, it's a head-over-head decision. Us humans are complicated. We chase what's bad for us and push away what isn't. Why is doing what's right for us so hard to do?
I could argue (along with the entire spiritual community) that we're drawn to certain people and situations to help us with our growth.

We are a curious species after all. If you didn't take that shot or make those choices, you'd end up living with regret even if not taking the path you chose would've saved you a lifetime of heartache.

Now to explain the title a little further.
When you experience heartbreak, your brain sends signals all over your body to your other organs. You feel pain in your heart but only because your brain felt it first.
When something doesn't align with you or goes against what you felt was your truth, you're left with an empty feeling. Your brain is trying to adjust to the new set of circumstances.
Finding the balance is key when this happens.
You cannot control others, you cannot control what they say, do or how they react.
However, you're in complete control of your reactions.

Our first instinct will always be to fall into a pattern that we are used to. We are so used to fighting our way through life, that when the time comes to act, we fight.
Not every action deserves a reaction. Your energy is sacred and you worked hard to get to the place you're at. Even if that place is simply just being alive for as long as you have.
The first step to balancing your emotions is to have control of your mind.

I have a 10-second rule. This allows me to process the situation before acting. I know that most people are just projecting their inner trauma onto me and that allows me to detach myself from the situation and look at it with more compassion.

Trust me, I've been through some pretty unforgivable situations and yet, the only one it was hurting was me. By not choosing to work through those repressed emotions, I was in reality choosing to live within them.
They controlled me.

My brain was stuck in these memories because I was never given the option to escape them. When I learned this, everything changed for me.

We need someone to blame. I chose to look at the situation in a different light and see what caused this event to take place. What led up to this point?
Who were the people involved and what were their stories?

To truly have clarity, you have to understand every aspect of the event. You aren't the only one hurt, and no I'm in no way making excuses for the villains of your past.
Although what they did inflicted pain on you, they have a story themselves, and maybe they too were acting out trauma without a second thought.

This clarity is where freedom lives. The terrible things that happened to you, made you who you are. Freedom lives within the understanding of all parties involved.

You don't have to like them, or speak to them again. I'm simply pointing out that the pain and hatred you hold onto is poison to yourself and in no way changes the outcome of their lives.

You're in control of yourself. Your life is completely up to the choices you make while you're here. I for one am very happy that you're here.

10 Chapter Points to remember

- Your brain is like a computer program
- Trauma responses or patterns
- Your heart hurts because your brain is adjusting
- Your first instinct is a pattern
- Others are acting out of pain too

Tip 11:

Although they never showed you, you come first.

Going back to the point I made in a previous tip, your first definition of love was given to you by your immediate family. You were given a set of rules to follow and learned very quickly what it meant to go against these rules.

Many of us were shown that other people's happiness comes before our own and that sacrifices made to please others were well worth it in the end. Let me ask you though, how many times have you made a sacrifice and given up on something you were dead set and passionate about and still felt good in the end? I can only name a couple, but that good feeling was only because the person I made the sacrifice for was happy and I knew I did that.

I still felt the same way about what I sacrificed.

I still wanted it badly enough to fight for it. It just got shoved down deep into the place I keep all my other wants and desires.

Oftentimes we think of this as a fair trade. We just forget that a desire repressed isn't a dead desire. Being true to yourself can hurt others' feelings. It's in our nature to be in a relationship with other people.

When we feel we did something to tarnish that or even destroy it, we second guess our plans and act in a way that suffocates our wishes to preserve those relationships.

The right people will accept you for who you are. The you that you become when you're truly yourself will be a beacon of light and inspiration for others secretly dealing with a similar situation.

Remember that people are afraid of change. They don't understand it so they panic.

Panic can look like a lot of different things. Some people are explosive, some get quiet, others nod and say their happiness for you all the while they speak badly about you because they don't understand why your old life wasn't working for you anymore.

I've come to offer you some hope and relief. It's not your job to protect the version of you others hold. It's not your job to be the person they see you as.

Everyone you've ever met has a different outlook on you. Those people that they created are not your responsibility.

Nobody can predict the future. The closest you get to predicting your own is the choices you make in your present. Besides, the present is the only time that matters.

It's okay to set boundaries. Boundaries are healthy. It took me many years to learn this but once I got it down, I felt so much more in control of my life and what happens in it.

By you taking the burden from somebody else, it's showing them that you don't believe they can carry it. You go around picking up other people's weight because it makes their life easier. In turn, it makes yours harder.

It's okay if you don't live the life your parents envisioned for you. It's okay if you like other things than your friends. It's okay if your children don't understand your choices.
You're an individual within a community of other people. You may relate to that community, love it and find a home within it but, you are still an individual. Your peace means so much. You always come first. If you aren't in a good place, how can you help anyone else?

11 Chapter Points to remember

- Sacrifice doesn't always equal happiness
- A desire repressed isn't a dead desire
- The right people accept you for who you are
- People are afraid of change
- Panic looks different in everyone
- Everyone you meet has a different outlook on you
- You are still an individual

Tip 12:

If it exists, it's possible, if it doesn't, it can be made

Every idea starts in your mind. Every great thing that has ever been created started as a thought.
You get thousands of great ideas throughout your life that if you built upon them, they'd be turned into physical things that would impact your life as well as the world in beautiful ways.

Think about this, before trains were invented, most people rode horses or even walked. Someone got tired of the way things were and decided to build upon a thought that started in their head.

Your ideas can impact the world in ways you never imagined. You were blessed with an idea on purpose, if you don't know how to make it a reality, either teach yourself or find someone who possesses the skills you need to do so.

Visionaries are important in our society.

People search for a sense of fulfillment and accomplishment. There's no better feeling than providing a solution to a problem, especially for a large group of people. So dream, imagine, and don't let your childlike imagination be suffocated by adult responsibilities.

Even small ideas can be built upon. Tiny fragments run through your mind that come in when you wonder how you can make your life easier. Hold onto the fragments, write them down or start a note on your phone. Allow yourself to imagine a life after your problem was solved. Finally, let the ideas run free and follow your intuitive nudges.

Intuitive nudges can look and feel like a lot of different things. Sometimes they can feel like they are 'knowing'.
To put this example into context, imagine your driving to work.
You take this same route every day, today you get an urge to take a turn that you don't normally take.

You have no idea why you need to take this turn other than a gut feeling and a 'knowing' that it is the right move to make.

This is the most common way your intuition will chime in. When you're in a situation and you can't put your finger on it but you know something is off.

Another common way for your intuition to send you nudges is to show you signs.
Signs can look like a lot of things.

Seeing the same number over and over, looking up at a billboard and seeing advertisements for something you're personally seeking advice on, a friend calling out of nowhere offering you gifts or advice that fit perfectly into the solution for your problem.

None of these are accidents. Although some would call them blessings. Trust the signs, trust your intuition and when they call, answer it.

Most of the time we have no idea what something could become until we decide to start taking the first step. All you have to do is take the first step. All of the other steps are like a web that makes up the end goal.

Taking the wrong steps is like trial and error or a process of elimination. You have to know the wrong way of doing something to figure out the right way of doing it.
Making those mistakes now saves you time and hassle in the future.

Don't be afraid to fall. Falling is a part of learning and learning is a part of success. You got this. Now step.

12 Chapter Points to remember

- Your ideas can impact the world
- Don't let your childlike imagination get suffocated by adult responsibilities
- Hold onto the fragments
- Intuitive nudges
- Nothing is an accident

Tip 13:

People are mean, but so were their parents

We've all met someone and thought, you're an ass. C'mon, I'm
not the only one to think so.
People are their experiences until they choose otherwise.
I guess in a way we still are our experiences. We have a choice,
every single one of us, to either let our pain rule our lives or fuel
our drive.

These people that you meet, 9 times out of 10 are just reacting to
their environment with bottled-up emotions that are craving to
be set free.
Everybody has a story, not everyone feels the same sense of
awareness as you do.

I'm not making excuses for people to act like complete jackasses because I still believe in people and leaving them better than you found them.
Not everyone thinks this way though. You know how it feels to live in a chaotic tornado of deep-rooted trauma and repeated letdowns. You've been in that place before.
Sometimes people are just having a bad day, sometimes just a bad life.

Remember that panic can manifest in many different ways, the most common form is anger.

Our bodies never truly forget the pain we experience. If you let these unresolved emotions fester long enough, they become a part of your personality. You will find many little reasons as to why you feel or act the way you do but honestly, these things started long ago and were left alone to build into this icky feeling you carry around every day of your life.

Sadly a lot of us never had good role models, we never learned what healthy love looked like and we're just doing the best we know how to do.
We get lost in the doom and gloom of life because as far as we are concerned, life hasn't given us enough goodness to make us change.

Do you remember being so full of anger for so long? Do you remember waking up every day expecting to be let down once again? They do too. Except they are currently experiencing what you've grown from.

The best thing you can do with these people is to show them compassion. Killing them with kindness isn't just something you're told to avoid drama.
Killing them with kindness is healing for yourself as well.

When you show compassion for someone who probably doesn't get a lot of it, you're slowly restoring hope in someone who thought they've all but lost any sight of it.
They learned to love from their families the same way you did. Some of them probably didn't have a family or wished they didn't. They are doing the best they can just like you.
That's not saying that you should roll over and take it, it's saying you are more in control of your emotional state than they are, you have the advantage. When you know you've won, you don't feel the need to compete anymore.

Your experience with this person doesn't change your life. It doesn't change the way you look at yourself or the people in this world. Hurt people, hurt people. You're simply just not playing the same game as them.

Yes, this will take some practice and you will slip from time to time. It doesn't make you a failure, it makes you human.

You aren't weak for showing someone that hurt you compassion. You just found a way to understand your pain enough to know others feel their own.
It isn't your job to fix them, but while you're in the experience, be true to your growth and know that you are in complete control of your emotions.

It's a bad day, not a bad life and hey, maybe your kindness is the thing they needed to restore hope in humanity.

78

13 Chapter Points to remember

- We are our experiences
- Leave people better than you found them
- Compound pain becomes a personality
- You don't know what someone else has gone through
- Heal them with kindness

Tip 14:

Any bond can be broken

Love is many things. Love can be the deepest pain you've ever experienced or the greatest high you've ever known.
A connection to someone you felt gave you what you were missing, for even a short amount of time, can completely alter your life.
The reality of it all is any bond, no matter how strong, can be broken.

We have pre-set boundaries that our life experiences made us set. When we fall into a strong connection with someone, we become more lenient with those boundaries.

We feel deep down that something doesn't align with us. We're so used to the rejection patterns of our past that we give up parts of ourselves to ensure the relationship stays alive, even though if it didn't stay alive it would probably benefit us more.

How many times have you heard," it's just how they are", "they don't mean it", and "their just upset". As excuses for disrespectful and degrading actions? The action doesn't change, your connection to the person alters your response to it.

When people get comfortable their true colors shine bright. Anybody can be fooled in the beginning. Don't beat yourself up too much if the person you met isn't the person you know today.

The longer you've known somebody, the harder it is to cope with their absence.

You were existing before them and probably had other connections that were important to you as well. Those past connections may seem less important now because you're in the moment, but at the time those connections mattered to you just as much.

We tend to attach our happiness to other people and when the relationship has run its course and the rose-colored glasses are no longer working, we feel the same void we started with.

The common denominator in all of this is you. Your void isn't attached to others, nor can it be fixed by them.
People and connections play an important part in our lives and unfortunately, our first examples of these were mostly toxic and habitual.

We are constantly searching for something to fill the void we've felt our entire lives, and most of the time we try to fill it with people. I'm guilty of this as well. Filling the void with people is similar to being a drug addict. Now, before the criticism comes let me elaborate a little bit.

When you search for validation from others what do you feel? A high? Euphoric? The way that addicts feel when they get their fix. The only difference is the thing you're addicted to. Addicts can be chaotic, and mess up their lives and relationships.

You in a toxic relationship do the same thing. You push people away that don't agree with your bond, lash out when they point it out to you, go to great lengths for this person and even change things about yourself and give part of your self-respect up in the process.

You both are looking for that high.

What do you gain from these relationships other than not being alone? Yes, the good times are great but the bad times, are terrible.

Healing starts with you. When you heal, you grow. When you grow, you change. When you change, so does your life.

Start at the source and start working through the issues that make you cling to people to fill the void, to begin with. At the end of that healing is your freedom.

The relationships that no longer serve you will fall away. The people who don't align and aren't for your highest good will as well. Don't panic, the "you" that you will be is thinking from a healthier mindset. Everything always works out in the end and if it's not working out then it's not the end.

14 Chapter Points to remember

- Love is many things
- Any bond, no matter how strong, can be broken
- Your connection to another person alters your response
- We attach our happiness to other people
- Heal yourself, change your life

Tip 15:

The self-destruct sequence

Ready, set, destruct.

For some reason, we have this internal yearning to destroy ourselves. If it feels good, we don't care about the effects it'll have on us.

This approach to life could be either good or bad. Good in the moment that we are experiencing something that brings us some sort of peace. Bad in the moments where this thing we enjoyed comes back and bites us in the ass.

Let's take smoking for instance. Smoking helps you calm your nerves, gives idle hands something to do, etc. At the same time, it can have fatal effects on your health.

I smoked for 13 years personally. It was the "lesser of evils" according to my father. Smoking was the tool that I used to get me off of the self-harm kick I was on. Smoking kept my hands busy. Smoking gave me an outlet for my anxiety and although I knew of the long-term health effects it would have on me, honestly, I didn't care as long as I felt good at the moment.

As hard as people try to play the teeter-totter game of "not too far in the past, not too far in the future" with their thoughts, if you think about it we do a lot at the moment living when we say "F it" and do what makes us feel good.

Why are we only guilty when the thing we say "F it" and do is good for us? If I had my bet, I'd say it had a lot to do with the oh-so-familiar pattern of pleasing people.

Self-destruction is a very common symptom of anxiety disorders. Self-destruction is how we cope with the isolation we feel inside of our environment. We place our physical being in harm's way while making our minds feel okay.

We sacrifice our bodies in the long term for peace of mind in the present. As long as we feel some sort of relief in the present, we don't care what the trade-off is. Even if the trade-off seems like making a deal with the devil.

When you feel overwhelmed, you go into panic mode or "Fight or flight". During fight or flight, the only thing you're seeking is perceived safety. With us being creatures of habit, we collect relationships, objects, and habits through our lives that bring us comfort, and when we are panicking we reach for them.

We know they aren't good for us, we know they make us somebody we don't necessarily like or resonate with but they make us feel safe while we have them.

We call it love, we make excuses for why we choose these things that make us feel terrible after we come down, but quite honestly we just use them as excuses not to deal with the emotions inside the isolation.

Everything that hurts, makes you grow. The growth doesn't start until after you let go. The fear of letting go mixed with the fear of the unknown keeps us in the self-destruction loop.

The key is to find comfort within. To listen to the feelings inside the loneliness and give them a voice. Your freedom is inside, many of us just aren't ready to have that talk.

15 Chapter Points to remember

- Internal yearning to destroy ourselves
- We do what makes us feel good
- Self-destruction is how we deal with the feeling of isolation
- Collecting comfort objects and people
- Everything that hurts us, makes us grow

Tip 16:

Change is hard, but so is staying put

Our internal guidance system is a mind-blowing thing. It can tell when something is off, tell you when danger is near, see through lies, and even tell you when it's time to move.
You'll always know when you've outgrown something. Most of us just don't listen.

As you may already know, we are creatures of habit. We settle into situations that give us a sense of safety, even if it's a false sense. Most of this is rooted in fear.
Fear will make all of your dreams seem like death traps. It's never the dream that's wrong, it's always our imagination intertwined with our trauma responses.

We can make up some pretty twisted scenarios in our heads. If we had someone talk to us the way we spoke to ourselves, we'd be ready to fight.

Why do we listen to the voice of nobody and allow it to control our lives and choices?
We know it's just our doubting mind talking to us but yet because it comes from inside we seem to trust it more.
We allow that doubting mind to talk us out of things that make our hearts sing and beat faster simultaneously.

New things are terrifying. That's a cold hard fact, but living an unfulfilling life is just as terrifying. Imagine the person you would be if you took those chances when they presented themselves.
We are all connected by this invisible energy that turns, twists and ties together but most of us are so wound up in our webs to notice the beauty in it.

When opportunities present themselves, a lot of momentum and puppeteering was put into it. You had a desire so strong that people who could assist you with it just fell from the sky and landed in your path.
These people don't always come with a lit-up sign that says, "I am the way to your goal".

Sometimes these people come as bread crumbs. You just have to trust that your intuition is guiding you to a place that you've asked to arrive at.

Most of us forget to enjoy the scenery while we're focused on our arrival. The best part of a road trip is the view.
What I mean by this is, that the journey to your goal will be the most memorable part of your story. If you just arrived where you're asking to be as soon as you asked for it, what would be life-changing about that? Where is the adventure in that?

Leaping is the scary part, the journey will be like a good book that you can't put down. Once you jump, you're on your way. The only thing stopping you from arriving is starting.
You can start in the smallest ways. Visualize your life as if you met your goal, buy small things for your business, talk about your plans, and get yourself excited.
Life can change in the blink of an eye, you've seen more than enough proof of this through your own experience.

You can talk yourself out of your dreams time and time again, tell yourself that you're happy and fulfilled all while you're holding onto a burning desire and life continues to do what it does best and changes anyways, or you can be brave and give yourself the chance that nobody else gave you. Leap, you'll either fall and get up or you'll fly. Either way, you'll get through it like you always do.

16 Chapter Points to remember

- You know when you've outgrown something
- It's never the dream that's wrong
- New things are terrifying but worth it
- It's the bread crumbs that lead to your goal
- LEAP

Tip 17:

The little things

You never know which moments will be life-defining until you've already lived through them.

We have this preconceived notion that the big dramatic moments are the ones that make the biggest impact on us. The big dramatic moments are the ones that we survived, the ones that we stressed through and did our best to escape. The life-defining moments, the ones that alter our worlds are the small ones.

Small moments are compiled into a mental film strip that is stored inside our minds.
Our bodies remember our physical and emotional reactions to life but our minds tend to remember the smallest blissful moments inside the chaos tornado.

When I was writing my first book, "The Deal", it was the small moments that made me change my mind from wanting to exit life, to instead appreciating the beauty of it. The book was supposed to be my autobiography and the reasoning for my early departure.

I know I'm not the only one who suffers from mental illness. This life will chew you up and spit you right back out, if you're Nero typical these days you're uncommon.

I'm not saying that your feelings aren't legitimate because they are. You don t have to justify your emotions to anyone or make excuses for feeling them, they're yours.

What I am saying is the little moments that make you laugh till you cry or find a new love for life and those you interact with are enough reasons to push through another day.
We're programmed to see the terrible over the good. We're programmed to notice the inconsistencies over the flow.
It's just the way our trauma brains work.

Just because you're in a whirlwind of darkness doesn't mean you're absent from light. You're just simply focusing on a part of the situation and settling into it.

I've had a very unfortunate childhood and a lot of trauma to go along with it. Oddly the memories I relive the most are the little things that made my childhood not as terrible as the stories.

Taking a moment even if it seems silly or completely random could be the exact thing that you need to completely change your perspective.

Sitting alone in the grass looking at nature for what it is. A beautiful, carefully constructed masterpiece. Everything has a place and interacts with its environment effortlessly. Humans are the only ones uncomfortable in our natural environment.

Walking away and doing something that has nothing to do with handling the situation but instead gives you a sense of peace and relaxation.

This allows you to reenter the situation in different energy and state of mind. We get so flustered and worked up because of the overwhelming nature of our life stresses. Enjoying the small things that bring a smile to your face is sometimes the best thing you can do for yourself and everyone involved.

Make a list of the things that make you feel peaceful. Petting an animal, your favorite tv show, your favorite people, meal, music, place.
When you feel yourself losing sight of the beauty of life, pick one and experience something new.
Your brain can't tell the difference between something you're experiencing and something your mind is convinced you're experiencing.

Reliving these memories that you emotionally connect to will do more for your mind and body than you think.
Feeling the warm summer breeze on your skin, laughing at a joke, sitting in a car eating your comfort food, talking to a friend.

These are the life-defining moments. These are the moments that make life worth it. When you're experiencing them, be present in them. When you need them, relive them. Your mind will thank you

17 Chapter Points to remember

- We don't know the important moments until their gone
- The little moments matter most
- We're programmed to notice inconsistencies
- Taking a moment can change your view
- Make a list of the things that make you feel good

Tip 18:

The importance of "Me" time

(Written By Briana Swoveland)

"Me" time, What is "me" time?
Sometimes me time is as simple as a bathroom break or sitting in your car for an extra five minutes.

"Me" time is as important as eating three times a day. It grounds you and gives you time to exhale that breath you didn't even know you were holding in.

Unplug from the world, hide from the kids, or in my case my pets. It's okay to not clean your house or do the laundry because you are just tired and just take a day to sleep or stay in bed.
Me time is just time for you. You're not selfish for taking time for yourself.

Do your hair, take a shower do what makes you feel good.

I didn't always have time, I would work a 9 or however long shift, come home, cook for the family and then try to get as much laundry done in two or three hours and then shower, bed, and repeat.

I was running myself ragged. One day I finally broke down to my husband and said I can't handle this, I need HELP!
He looked at me and said your next day off is about you. I had a very hard time with this.

You know that thing called mom guilt. Well, I have this thing I call wife guilt. I felt like I had to get these things done and if I didn't I failed, I felt like I failed the family and my husband.

It took a while for me to understand that I didn't have to complete each task, if I didn't make dinner it was okay that's what frozen hot pockets are for.

My "Me" time started on a Sunday morning.

My husband had to work three hours before I did so I dropped him off as I was driving. I was hungry but I didn't want the typical fast-food breakfast.

 I decided to have a good breakfast before work so I decided to eat by myself. I sat down, ordered my favorites, ate, and read my book which I had been trying to read for a month.

 It was the best fifteen dollars I ever spent. After that, I decided to take my time whenever I needed to.
It started with small things like doing my makeup and hair. Then it moved to get dressed up for no reason.

The smallest things can mean the most to you and your inner peace.
Do more things that make you smile just to do them.
They will greatly improve the quality of your life.

18 Chapter Points to remember

- Your nct selfish for taking time for yourself
- It's normal to feel guilt but it doesn't make it wrong
- Small things make a huge difference in your mental health

Tip 19:

You're stronger than you think

Think back to a time that changed your life. That painful memory that you store away deep inside your psyche can crush you in an instant.

You never thought you'd live through that. You never imagined yourself being well afterward, getting through life, let alone on a journey of healing and self-discovery.

Look at you, alive, breathing, and healing.

We don't give ourselves nearly enough credit for the pain that we endure. We see it as, "that's life I guess".

You are a warrior. You are brave and your voice is powerful beyond measure. If you've ever been in love you know how much words can alter moods and even lives. You've taken hits from every side and got back up swinging. Sometimes, getting up is the hardest part.

You've survived more than you realize, and are far braver than you give yourself credit for.
If you read your biography through the eyes of another you'd be hooked, fall in love with the character, and admire their strength and resilience.

We are so used to looking for that admiration and validation from outside of ourselves, if we don't hear it often from those around us we don't believe it to be true.
Just because it isn't plastered on the walls doesn't mean it isn't the most accurate statement ever. uttered.

Giving ourselves motivation and reassurance can be the hardest thing to learn. It feels like a chore, a lie, honestly, at first you feel like you're a terrible person trying to talk yourself into believing false statements.

If you would sit down and write down the things you've survived, you'd be amazed at yourself. All of the things that you truly thought would end you, didn't.

Going as far back as you can remember, think hard about it.
Now, look at where you are now. Aren't you proud? You don't have to
be a millionaire with thousands of fans to be successful. You lived
through situations designed to test you in every possible way. That's a
success.

You just roll with the punches and keep going. You're good at that.
Yes, you get tired. Yes, sometimes you need to rest.
All of those are natural responses. You aren't any less brave for
needing to breathe or take a break. The point is, you made it. Against
all odds you made it. You may not be in the same shape you were
when you started but that's okay. You aren't the best you yet. You are a
work in progress.
Thank yourself for all of those years of support. Love yourself for the
years of abuse you gave yourself. Let yourself rest from the years of
wear and tear. Take a moment and be present. You are amazing. You
are a hero. And you deserve all the good things in this world.

Strength isn't just a physical thing. Sometimes strength is waking up when you've been going for weeks and need a break.

Strength is eating something when you can't find the energy to live your life.

Strength is being supportive to someone you love even when the actions they took during their breakdown hurt you to the core.

Strength is being a full-time parent when you're not even sure what day it is.

Strength is walking away from a toxic relationship.

Strength is starting over all over again.

Strength is saying no to someone you love.

Strength is starting a project you've put off.

Strength is keeping your home together and in one piece.

Strength is loving again after a heartbreak.

Strength is burying a loved one and still moving forward with life.

Strength is teaching yourself how to be a functional adult when you never had a role model.

Strength is crying when you need to cry.

Strength is being afraid and doing it anyway.

Strength is getting back up after you've had your face pushed to the ground.

Strength is smiling when you want to cry.

You're strong in a lot of ways. And braver than you think.

19 Chapter Points to remember

- You survived what you thought you wouldn't
- Your voice is powerful beyond measure
- You don't give yourself enough credit
- Strength can be many things

Tip 20:

It kills others, it'll save you.

You've lived through some tough situations. Some of those you
didn't think you'd survive through.
You can look anywhere and find a list of people and their stories
that tell a tale of sadness and loss of hope.

Others lived through similar situations and let those moments
be the straw that broke the camel's back. Instead of crumbling,
as hard as it may have been, took those moments and used them
as fuel.
You were built for this. Built to fight, built to find hope in the
most hopeless set of circumstances.

You have something special within you, when you're facing darkness you forget that it's there. This invisible force keeps you going. The will to live.

Most times we don't even know why we have it, why it's so strong and why we even feel obligated to let it lead when everything else in our lives tells us not to.
We simply survive.

We're good at surviving. It's the first skill we learned as traumatized children.
Others' downfalls are the skills we carried with us through our lives.

It's truly amazing to think about it. Our minds and bodies take so much abuse throughout our lives that we just adapt to it and whether you realize it or not, let it fuel us.

When you got rejected, something magical happened. You developed this "I'll show you" attitude that fueled you to meet your goals.

When you got your heart broken, you became more aware of
your emotions and used a balance of logic and heart to make
future decisions.
When you lost someone you loved dearly, you cherished
everyone else in your life.

We don't even realize our greatest superpower.
We get so lost in the pain that we forget the positives of having
it.
Any negative emotion can be your superpower if you learn to
use it correctly.

Anger is the same energetic frequency as determination.
Sadness is the same energetic frequency as compassion or
sympathy.
Anxiousness is the same energetic frequency as excitement.

It's the way you use the energy. It's the thought behind the
emotion.

Instead of wanting to destroy everything in your path when you're mad, get hyper-focused on a goal. With the same intensity as the anger you feel.
When you're sad, use that as fuel to be compassionate for yourself as you would a friend going through the same situation.
When you're anxious, think about something that makes you excited and focus on that.

Everything has two sides or degrees.
Choose a different thought. You are completely in control of your reaction to things. You are completely in control of your emotions.

You feel the way you feel because how else would you know if something is for you or not?
This internal guidance system uses our emotions to help guide us through life.
Listen to it.

You are okay. You've survived worse, and it'll take practice but once you realize your thoughts at any moment control the way you feel, you'll find the freedom I've come to know so well.

20 Chapter Points to remember

- You used bad situations as fuel
- You have something special inside you
- Your experience is your greatest superpower
- Everything has to degrees
- Your thoughts at any moment, control how you feel

Epilogue

So, humans are confusing aren't they? We're all just bopping around doing the best we know how to do.
We all cry, love, and experience pain, sorrow, joy, and excitement.
We all get nervous, lost, and confused.

We aren't so different after all. We just have our ways of hiding it.
Hopefully what you've read in this book can help you navigate this crazy place a little better.
I hope that you'll find a sense of freedom while understanding yourself a little better.

We're all here. Now what? We just do the best we can to enjoy our experience as difficult as it may be at times.

Love is the only thing that matters. Self-love, love for family and friends, love for passion and life.

Your trauma is the biggest setback in your life. You are the only one who can change that narrative. You alone are in control of every choice you make. You alone are in control of the outcome of your life.
I believe in you enough for both of us.

I experienced my trauma for a reason. Part of that reason was to go through everything I've talked about in this book. I shared my healing journey with you all, my healing journey found you and hopefully sparked yours.

That's a good enough reason for me. If my story can help save one life, it's worth a whole lot more than the pain I experienced to get to this place of peace.

Your story isn't over. You aren't your age, you aren't your experiences, you aren't your bad thoughts or mistakes. You are human, And because you're human I love you.

You got this little soul, keep going. If you ever need these words again they'll be right here where you left them. If you feel the need to pass this book along to someone else who may need it, please do so.

We are all in this together, on a floating rock in space exchanging paper for labor.

Until next time,

C. Alexander

www.ingramcontent.com/pod-product-compliance
Lightning Source LLC
Chambersburg PA
CBHW020324290526
45785CB00007B/2915